Navajo Code Talkers

by Andrew Santella

Content Advisers: Navajo Code Talkers' Association,
Window Rock, Arizona
Roberta John, Navajo author,
Window Rock, Arizona

Reading Adviser: Dr. Linda D. Labbo,
Department of Reading Education, College of Education,
The University of Georgia

COMPASS POINT BOOKS
MINNEAPOLIS, MINNESOTA

Compass Point Books
1710 Roe Crest Drive
North Mankato, MN 56003

Printed in the United States of America in Stevens Point, Wisconsin.
072013
007515R

On the cover: Navajo code talkers Henry Bahe Jr. (left) and George H. Kirk served with the Marines in the South Pacific. They are operating a portable radio in a clearing they've hacked in the dense jungle in 1943.

Photographs ©: United States Marine Corps/Getty Images, cover; AFP/Getty Images, 4, 25, 40; National Archives, 5, 8, 10, 15, 21, 24, 37, 39; Nevada Weir/Corbis, 6; Franklin D. Roosevelt Library, 7; Underwood & Underwood/Corbis, 9; Northern Arizona University/Special Collections and Archives, 11, 20, 22, 30; Bettmann/Corbis, 12, 35; Hulton/Archive by Getty Images, 16; Kevin Fleming/Corbis, 17; Western History Department/Denver Public Library, 18; Special Collections, J. Willard Marriott Library, University of Utah, 19; Loomis Dean/Time Life Pictures/Getty Images, 23; Courtesy of Museum of Northern Arizona Photo Archives neg. #MS-136-4-3, 28; Courtesy of Museum of Northern Arizona Photo Archives neg. #MS-136-4-1, 31; DVIC/NARA, 33, 34; Dave G. Houser/Corbis, 38; The United States Mint, 41.

Editor: Catherine Neitge
Photo Researcher: Svetlana Zhurkina
Designer/Page Production: Bradfordesign, Inc./Biner Design
Cartographer: XNR Productions, Inc.

Library of Congress Cataloging-in-Publication Data
Santella, Andrew.
   Navajo code talkers / by Andrew Santella.
      p. cm. — (We the people)
   Includes index.
   ISBN 978-0-7565-0611-7 (hardcover)
   ISBN 978-0-7565-1020-6 (paperback)
   1. United States. Marine Corps—Indian troops—Juvenile literature. 2. World War, 1939-1945—Cryptography—Juvenile literature. 3. World War, 1939-1945—Participation, Indian—Juvenile literature. 4. Navajo Indians—Juvenile literature. [1. Cryptography. 2. Navajo Indians. 3. Indians of North America—Southwest, New.] I. Title. II. Series: We the people (Compass Point Books)
   D810.C88S26 2004
   940.54'8673—dc22   2003014438

Visit Compass Point Books on the Internet at *www.compasspointbooks.com*
or e-mail your request to *custserv@compasspointbooks.com*

TABLE OF CONTENTS

NOTE: *In this book, words that are defined in the glossary are in* **bold** *the first time they appear in the text.*

SPEAKING THE LANGUAGE

At Roy Hawthorne's school, there was one sure way to get in trouble. Hawthorne lived on the Navajo **reservation** in New Mexico in the 1930s and attended a school run by the United States government. Students at the school were

Former code talkers Roy Hawthorne (left) and John Brown Jr. attend the premiere of the 2002 movie "Windtalkers," which tells their story.

4

strictly forbidden to speak their native Navajo language. If they spoke anything other than English, they would likely have their mouths washed out with soap.

Hawthorne never stopped speaking Navajo, though. At home and at play, he still used the language that had been passed down through many Navajo generations. Years later, Hawthorne's knowledge of the Navajo language paid off for him and for his country. Hawthorne became a code talker.

A Navajo Marine uses his walkie-talkie during World War II in the South Pacific.

5

A former code talker marches in a Navajo parade in Window Rock, Arizona.

The code talkers were a group of about 400 Navajos who served in the United States Marine Corps during World War II (1939–1945). Their job was to send and receive secret coded messages. The code talkers invented a code that was never broken by the enemy. The code helped the United States and its allies win the war. The code they invented was based on the Navajo language—the same language that once got Navajo children like Roy Hawthorne in trouble.

6

A WORLD AT WAR

On December 7, 1941, Japanese forces attacked the U.S. naval base at Pearl Harbor in Hawaii. The next day, the United States declared war on Japan, and U.S. forces were soon at war around the world. Some of the fiercest fighting of World War II took place in the Pacific Ocean. U.S. forces there had been badly damaged by the attack on Pearl Harbor. In the early days of the war, the U.S. forces in the Pacific fought just

The Japanese attacked Pearl Harbor on December 7, 1941.

to survive the waves of Japanese attacks. The fighting extended across huge stretches of ocean. American planes, ships, and troops might be spread out across hundreds of miles of water. Victory depended upon the ability to quickly communicate battle plans and other important information over long distances.

By the 1940s, the military had developed new wireless radios that could send and receive messages. They were bulky and heavy, but they allowed troops to stay in almost constant contact with other friendly forces. The trouble was, the enemy could hear these radio conversations, too. The Japanese military used groups of English-speaking soldiers to listen in on American military radio messages.

Code talkers Preston Toledo (left) and his cousin Frank Toledo send coded messages over a wireless radio.

Members of the Japanese Army listen in on radio broadcasts during a training session in World War II.

The Japanese hoped to learn details about American defenses or troop movements. They hoped to get advance warning of American plans. The U.S. military would develop codes to make it more difficult for the enemy to understand their messages. However, enemy **code breakers** would figure out these codes, and then new ones were needed. Some American codes became so complicated that it could take hours to translate messages. By then, it might be too late to act on the messages.

What was needed was a simple, but unbreakable, code. The solution came not from the military, but from a Los Angeles engineer named Philip Johnston. He was the son of missionaries who had spent years working with the Navajos. Though Johnston wasn't a Navajo himself, he had grown up on a Navajo reservation and he knew the Navajo language well. Johnston had read about the military's efforts to develop secret codes. He believed that a code based on the Navajo language would be almost impossible to break.

A Navajo family stands in front of their home in the mid-1930s.

PHILIP JOHNSTON'S IDEA

Johnston was one of just a few non-Navajos who could speak and understand the Navajo language. He knew from personal experience how hard it was for non-Navajos to learn the language. In Navajo, each syllable carries meaning and must be pronounced just right if the speaker hopes to be understood. Even the tone of the speaker's voice communicates different meanings. The slightest mistake in tone or pronunciation can change the meaning of a word or sentence completely. All these factors make Navajo a very difficult language to master. Even people who speak other Native American languages have been baffled by Navajo. The more

Philip Johnston (right) talks with a Navajo friend in 1941.

11

Johnston thought about it, the more certain he became that a code based on Navajo could be just what the military was looking for.

Johnston contacted Marine Corps offices in southern California and eventually arranged a meeting with Major James E. Jones. The officer listened politely to Johnston's ideas, but at first they seemed like nothing new. In World War I, the Army had used Choctaw soldiers to send and translate secret messages by phone. They also recruited Sac, Fox, Chippewa, and Oneida messengers for duty in World War II. However, military leaders knew that even students from other countries, including Japan

Army Private Floyd Dann speaks in his native Hopi language to send messages in 1943.

and Germany, had begun to study Native American languages. The more non-native people learned about Native American languages, the less useful these languages would be for secret communications.

In response to Jones's doubts, Johnston explained how the Navajo language could be used to create a code. First, he said the Navajo language was not as well understood as other Native American languages. Even if enemy code breakers could understand other languages, they would likely be puzzled by Navajo. Then Johnston explained that he proposed not simply sending secret messages in Navajo, but creating a code based on the Navajo language. The combined difficulty of understanding Navajo and cracking the code would make it almost impossible for the enemy to understand the secret communications. Johnston also told Jones that the size of the Navajo Nation would work to the advantage of U.S. forces. At the start of World War II, the Navajo Nation numbered about 50,000 people, large enough to provide plenty of translators for the military.

13

A map of the Navajo reservation and surrounding area

Johnston's presentation convinced Jones. In
March 1942, he arranged for Johnston to meet with
Major General Clayton Vogel and Colonel Wethered
Woodward from U.S. Marines headquarters in

Washington, D.C. Johnston sold them on the idea, too, and the top leadership of the Marines agreed to give Johnston's plan a tryout. The Marines would recruit a group of Navajos, who would develop a code using their language. The next task was to find Navajos who would turn Johnston's idea into reality.

HEADQUARTERS,
AMPHIBIOUS FORCE, PACIFIC FLEET,
CAMP ELLIOTT, SAN DIEGO, CALIFORNIA

March 6, 1942

From: The Commanding General.
To: The Commandant, U. S. Marine Corps.

Subject: Enlistment of Navaho Indians.

Enclosures: (A) Brochure by Mr. Philip Johnston, with maps.
            (B) Messages used in demonstration.

1.   Mr. Philip Johnston of Los Angeles recently offered his services to this force to demonstrate the use of Indians for the transmission of messages by telephone and voice-radio. His offer was accepted and the demonstration was held for the Commanding General and his staff.

2.   The demonstration was interesting and successful. Messages were transmitted and received almost verbatim. In conducting the demonstration messages were written by a member of the staff and handed to the Indian; he would transmit the message in his tribal dialect and the Indian on the other end would write them down in English. The text of messages as written and received are enclosed. The Indians do not have many military terms in their dialect so it was necessary to give them a few minutes, before the demonstration, to improvise words for dive-bombing, anti-tank gun, etc.

3.   Mr. Johnston stated that the Navaho is the only tribe in the United States that has not been infested with German students during the past twenty years. These Germans, studying the various tribal dialects under the guise of art students, anthropologists, etc., have undoubtedly attained a good working knowledge of all tribal dialects except Navaho. For this reason the Navaho is the only tribe available offering complete security for the type of work under consideration. It is noted in Mr. Johnston's article (enclosed) that the Navaho is the largest tribe but the lowest in literacy. He stated, however, that 1,000 — if that many were needed — could be found with the necessary qualifications. It should also be noted that the Navaho tribal dialect is completely unintelligible to all other tribes and all other people, with the possible exception of as many as 28 Americans who have made a study of the dialect. This dialect is thus equivalent to a secret code to the enemy, and admirably suited for rapid, secure communication.

15/11-jwa

Subject: Enlistment of Navaho Indians.

- -

4.   It is therefore recommended that an effort be made to enlist 200 Navaho Indians for this force. In addition to linguistic qualifications in English and their tribal dialect they should have the physical qualifications necessary for messengers.

CLAYTON B. VOGEL

Copy to CG, AFAF.

General Vogel's letter recommending the code talker project

THE NAVAJO

To find Navajos to enlist in the Marines' code program, **recruiters** traveled to the Navajo reservation. The largest in the United States, the Navajo reservation stretches across parts of Utah, Arizona, and New Mexico. It is about the size of the state of West Virginia. Within the boundaries of the reservation, the Marine recruiters found a unique world with its own traditions, its own language, and its own culture.

Navajos herd sheep on the reservation in Monument Valley, Arizona.

16

Navajos once lived in Canada and were part of a group of native people called the Athabascans. About 1,000 years ago, they split off and began moving south. Eventually, they settled in the dry country that is now their home. According to their legends, spirits instructed them to settle in a land surrounded by four mountains. The Navajo people were told that as long as they lived in this place, they would be safe. To the Navajos, the land they call home is sacred.

Shiprock is a spiritual symbol of the Navajo Nation.

17

They defended their land fiercely when the U.S. Army arrived in 1848 to occupy it. In the 1850s, a Navajo leader named Manuelito led a lengthy and bloody war against the U.S. Army, but could not drive away the new-

comers. In 1864, forces led by Colonel Kit Carson finally subdued the Navajos. About 8,500 Navajos captured in northeast Arizona were forced to walk more than 300 miles to Fort Sumner in eastern New Mexico. The forced march to **Bosque Redondo** near Fort Sumner became known to the Navajo people as the Long Walk. Many

Manuelito in the late 1800s

18

A Navajo woman with her baby on her back during their captivity at Bosque Redondo

Navajos did not survive it. Those who did make it to Fort Sumner found themselves held captive in a strange land.

In 1868, the U.S. government finally allowed the Navajos to return to their homeland, which the government had turned into a reservation. Still, the government tried to force the Navajos to give up their traditional ways and to adopt European ways instead. Government schools forbade the use of the Navajo language.

19

Their long history of harsh treatment by the U.S. government did not stop the Navajos from answering their country's call during World War II. In fact, Marine recruiters at the reservation met long lines of candidates in 1942. The Navajo code project was top secret, so the Navajos didn't know they were signing up to be code talkers. They knew only that they were joining the Marines and helping to defend the United States. Some Navajos who were still in their early teens told recruiters they were 18, the minimum age for Marines. One was accepted even though he was really just 15. None of the Navajos knew what awaited them as Marines.

Marine recruiters toured the Navajo reservation in 1942.

MILITARY TRAINING

The first task for any new Marine is completing the Marine Corps training course, sometimes called boot camp. In May 1942, the new Marines from the Navajo reservation were sent to the Marine Corps Recruit Training Depot in San Diego. For many, the trip west marked their first time on a bus. Some had never left the reservation before. Most had never been in a big city. Like most Marines, they struggled to complete the seven exhausting weeks of training.

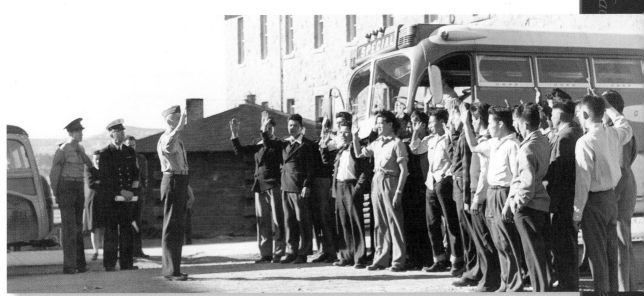

The original 29 code talkers were sworn in at Fort Wingate, New Mexico, in 1942.

21

The Navajo Marine recruits marched in formation during their training in California.

In the training course, Marine recruits endure difficult physical fitness tests. They complete long marches carrying heavy packs. They spend hour after hour practicing basic drills. The goal is to make the training course so difficult that it will turn new recruits into disciplined Marines who are ready for anything. Marine training instructors were surprised to find that the Navajos had little trouble with the fitness tests. Many had grown up herding sheep and hauling water on ranches. They were used to hard work and exercise. However, other parts of boot camp were more difficult to get used to.

In some ways, the training course clashed with Navajo traditions. Many Navajos wore their hair in thick braids, but as Marine recruits they had to shave off their hair. Marine drill instructors insisted on looking directly into the eyes of recruits, but in the Navajo culture this is considered rude. Even wearing a military uniform seemed foreign to some of the Navajos. Despite the difficulties, the 29 Navajos completed boot camp and graduated to the next step in their training. They were about to become code talkers.

The Navajo reservation in the 1940s

CREATING THE CODE

After boot camp, the Navajos were sent to Camp Elliott, a Marine Corps post in Southern California. There, they received training in radio communications and basic electronics. They learned to use, care for, and repair the radios that would send their coded messages. Only at Camp Elliott did it become clear to the Navajos what their special mission would be. Finally, it came time to create the unbreakable code.

Barracks at Camp Elliott in 1942

Chester Nez (left) received a congressional gold medal from President Bush in 2001.

A Navajo code talker named Chester Nez later recalled how the code came to be. "We were told to use our language to come up with words representing each letter, from A to Z," he explained. "And they also told us to

25

Sample of the Navajo Dictionary

English Letter	Navajo Word	Meaning
A	Wol-la-chee	Ant
B	Shush	Bear
C	Ba-goshi	Cow
D	Lha-cha-eh	Dog
E	Dzeh	Elk
F	Ma-e	Fox
G	Ah-tad	Girl
H	Lin	Horse
I	Tkin	Ice
J	Yil-doi	Jerk
K	Klizzie-yazzie	Kid
L	Ah-jad	Leg
M	Na-as-tso-si	Mouse
N	A-chin	Nose
O	Ne-ahs-jah	Owl
P	Bi-so-dih	Pig
Q	Ca-yeilth	Quiver
R	Gah	Rabbit
S	Klesh	Snake
T	A-woh	Tooth
U	Shi-da	Uncle
V	A-keh-di-glini	Victor
W	Gloe-ih	Weasel
X	Al-na-as-dzoh	Cross
Y	Tsah-as-zih	Yucca
Z	Besh-do-tliz	Zinc

English Word	Navajo Word	Meaning
Corps	Din-neh-ih	Clan
Switchboard	Ya-ih-e-tih-ih	Central
Dive bomber	Gini	Chicken hawk
Torpedo plane	Tas-chizzie	Swallow
Observation plane	Ne-as-jah	Owl
Fighter plane	Da-he-tih-hi	Hummingbird
Bomber	Jay-sho	Buzzard
Alaska	Beh-hga	With winter
America	Ne-he-mah	Our mother
Australia	Cha-yes-desi	Rolled hat
Germany	Besh-be-cha-he	Iron hat
Philippines	Ke-yah-da-na-lhe	Floating island

Source: Naval Historical Center

26

come up with code words for military terms. They put us all in a room to work it out and at first everyone thought we'd never make it. It seemed impossible, because even among ourselves, we didn't agree on all the right words."

However, the Navajos devised a code that worked extremely well. They made a list of Navajo words that would represent each letter in the English language alphabet. For example, the Navajo word for apple (*be-la-sana*) stood for the letter A. The Navajo word for bear (*shush*) stood for the letter B, and the Navajo word for cat (*moasi*) stood for the letter C. The code talkers sent messages by using Navajo code words to spell out words in English. For example, to say "Navy," code talkers would say the Navajo words that stood for each letter: *Nesh-chee* (or nut, for N), *wol-la-chee* (or ant, for A), *a-keh-di-glini* (or victor, for V), and *tsah-as-zih* (or yucca, for Y).

Later, the Navajos made the code more difficult to crack by adding more code words. Some English letters could be represented by as many as three different Navajo

27

words. For example, for the letter A, code talkers could use *wol-la-chee* (ant), *be-la-sana* (apple), or *tse-nill* (ax).

Not all words had to be spelled out letter by letter, however. The code talkers came up with a list of Navajo words or phrases that could be used to represent common

Jimmie King played a drum as he and three of his fellow Navajo Marines prepared to entertain other recruits at Camp Elliott in 1942.

28

military terms. Many of these code words came from the Navajo knowledge of the natural world. Fighter planes flew quickly and made a buzzing noise, so they were given the code name *dah-he-tih-hi,* which is the Navajo word for hummingbird. Dive bombers were named for chicken hawks, or *gini.* The bombs they dropped were given the code name *a-ye-shi,* the Navajo word for eggs.

Battleships were called *lo-tso,* or whales in Navajo. Submarines were called *besh-lo,* which translates as iron fish. The code word for the United States was *ne-he-mah,* which means "our mother" in Navajo.

To start with, the code had about 200 such words, but by the end of the war it had grown to include about 600 words. The code talkers had to memorize the entire code before being shipped out for active duty. To keep the code secret, no written lists were allowed outside Marine training centers. Code talkers also practiced sending and translating messages quickly. They practiced

Philip Johnston (right) with five Navajos who served as instructors at Camp Elliott. They are (from left) Johnny Manuelito, John Benally, Rex Knotz, Howard Billiman, and Peter Tracy.

until they could send and translate a three-line message in just 20 seconds. Most important of all, they learned to send and translate messages without errors. The slightest mistake could change the meaning of a message and place troops in danger.

30

Marine Corps leaders were so pleased with the code that they expanded the code talker program. Philip Johnston was placed in charge of recruiting more Navajos. Some came from the reservation, and some transferred to the Marines from other branches of the armed forces. From the original 29 code talkers, the program grew to include about 400 Navajos.

Philip Johnston (left) with Corporal Johnny Manuelito

ON THE BATTLEFIELD

By the summer of 1942, the first Navajo code talkers were ready to join troops at the front line. Between 1942 and 1945, code talkers took part in most of the major battles fought in the Pacific Ocean. United States and allied forces were able to stop Japanese advances. Then, in a series of bloody battles for control of islands in the Pacific, the Japanese were finally driven back and defeated.

Code talkers were often in the middle of the heaviest fighting. They were usually among the first wave of troops to storm enemy positions. They carried their bulky radios and set them up while under intense fire from the enemy. They reported the location of enemy forces, sent word on the progress of allied forces, and made requests for **reinforcements.** With bullets flying all around them, the code talkers worked calmly to send and receive the information that helped ensure victory. Often they worked in foxholes, or shallow trenches they dug for protection from

Navajo code talkers were among the first Marines to land on Saipan in June 1944

33

Marines raised the flag at Iwo Jima on February 23, 1945.

enemy fire. At the key battle of Iwo Jima, six code talkers worked day and night to send more than 800 messages. They made not a single mistake. Later, Marine Major Howard Connor said, "Were it not for the Navajo, the Marines would have never taken Iwo Jima."

The code worked exactly as the Marines had hoped. When the enemy was able to listen in on American radio conversations, they failed to understand anything being said. All they heard were noises that sounded like no language they knew. The Japanese never broke the Navajo code. In one battle report, Marine Captain Ralph Stuckey said that the code talkers were "the simplest, fastest and most reliable means available" to send secret orders.

Navajo code talkers Henry Bahe Jr. (left) and George H. Kirk send messages on a portable radio in the dense jungle.

35

BACK HOME

Japan's surrender in 1945 brought an end to the fighting in the Pacific Ocean. The work of the code talkers was complete. Of the 400 or so Navajos who served as code talkers, 13 had died in action. At the end of the war, the survivors were instructed to not talk about their jobs. The Marines wanted to keep the Navajo code a secret, in case it had to be used again in future conflicts. As a result, very few people knew of the remarkable role the code talkers had played in World War II. They received no special recognition or honors. Instead, they quietly resumed their lives on the reservation.

Not until 1969 did military officials reveal the secret of the Navajo code talkers. Slowly, interest in the story of the code talkers grew. In 1982, President Ronald Reagan declared August 14 National Navajo

Navajo code talkers, including these Marines who landed on Bougainville in the Solomon Islands, did not discuss their jobs after the war.

37

A sculpture by artist R. C. Gorman honoring the Navajo code talkers stands on the campus of Northern Arizona University.

Code Talker Day. In 2000, Senator Jeff Bingaman of New Mexico proposed an act honoring the code talkers. President Bill Clinton signed the act into law on December 22, 2000.

Code talker Carl Gorman, shown in 1944 on Saipan, served as the model for his son's Arizona sculpture.

On July 26, 2001, President George W. Bush awarded Congressional gold medals to each of the 29 original code talkers. The families of code talkers who had died accepted their medals during a ceremony in the

John Brown Jr. receives a congressional gold medal from President Bush at the Capitol in 2001.

Capitol. Only five of the original 29 were still alive to receive the awards at the Washington, D.C., ceremony. The code talkers "brought honor to their nation and victory to their country," said President Bush.

Later that year, silver medals were awarded to every Navajo code talker during ceremonies in Window Rock, Arizona. "All Americans owe these great men a debt of gratitude," said Senator Ben Nighthorse Campbell of Colorado. Long after they had bravely served their country, the Navajo code talkers were finally taking their place in history.

A bronze copy shows both sides of the medal awarded to the code talkers. The Navajo words at the bottom mean "The Navajo language was used to defeat the enemy."

41

GLOSSARY

Bosque Redondo—area on the Pecos River named for a grove of cottonwood trees; it served as a prison camp for more than 8,000 Navajos and 500 Mescalero Apache in the 1860s

code breakers—people who try to figure out how a code works so that secret messages can be understood

recruiters—people who sign up new members of the military services

reinforcements—a new supply of troops to strengthen a military force

reservation—a large area of land set aside for Native Americans

DID YOU KNOW?

- Window Rock, Arizona, is the capital of the Navajo Nation.

- The Navajos planted more than 10,000 cottonwood trees at Bosque Redondo to supply them with firewood. About 35 of those trees still stand today.

- In 1968, a group of Navajos returned to Fort Sumner to reenact the signing of the 1868 peace treaty that allowed the Navajos to return home. A marker was placed near the site, and Navajos leave stones there in memory of the Long Walk. The state of New Mexico is planning a multimillion dollar Bosque Redondo Memorial museum and visitor center at the site.

IMPORTANT DATES

Timeline

1864	U.S. Army defeats Navajos and forces many to make the 300-mile Long Walk to Fort Sumner.
1868	Navajos allowed to move to new reservation on their traditional homeland.
1941	Japanese attack on Pearl Harbor brings United States into World War II.
1942	First code talkers train and begin serving in the Pacific Ocean.
1945	Japan's surrender ends World War II.
1982	President Ronald Reagan declares National Navajo Code Talker Day.
2000	Congress passes law honoring code talkers.
2001	President George W. Bush awards gold medals to 29 original code talkers; silver medals are awarded to all code talkers.

IMPORTANT PEOPLE

DR. SAMUEL BILLISON (1926–)
World War II code talker and president of Navajo Code Talkers' Association

JEFF BINGAMAN (1943–)
Democratic senator from New Mexico who sponsored legislation honoring the code talkers

PHILIP JOHNSTON (1892–1978)
Son of missionaries who grew up on the Navajo reservation and convinced the military to use a code based on the Navajo language

MANUELITO (1818–1893)
Navajo warrior who led his people against the U.S. Army but eventually surrendered and went to Bosque Redondo; he was one of the signers of the 1868 peace treaty that allowed the Navajo to return to their homeland

WANT TO KNOW MORE?

At the Library

Aaseng, Nathan. *Navajo Code Talkers.* New York: Walker, 2002.

Durrett, Deanne. *Unsung Heroes of World War II: The Story of the Navajo
Code Talkers.* New York: Facts on File, 1998.

On the Web

For more information on this topic, use FactHound.

1. Go to *www.facthound.com*

2. Type in this book ID: 0756506115

3. Click on the *Fetch It* button.

FactHound will find the best Web sites for you.

Through the Mail

Navajo Code Talkers' Association

P.O. Box 1182

Window Rock, AZ 86515

To contact the official group that represents the Navajo code talkers

On the Road

Navajo Code Talkers Room

Gallup/McKinley County Chamber of Commerce

103 W. Highway 66

Gallup, NM 87301

505/722-2228

To see photos and other memorabilia honoring the Navajo code talkers

National Cryptologic Museum

National Security Agency

Maryland Route 32 and the Baltimore/Washington Parkway

Fort Meade, MD 20755

301/688-5849

To view an exhibit on Native American code talkers

Fort Sumner State Monument

Fort Sumner, NM 88119

505/355-7705

To visit the site where the Navajo people were imprisoned after the Long Walk

INDEX

About the Author

Andrew Santella writes for magazines and newspapers, including GQ and the New York Times Book Review. He is the author of a number of books for young readers. He lives outside Chicago with his wife and son.